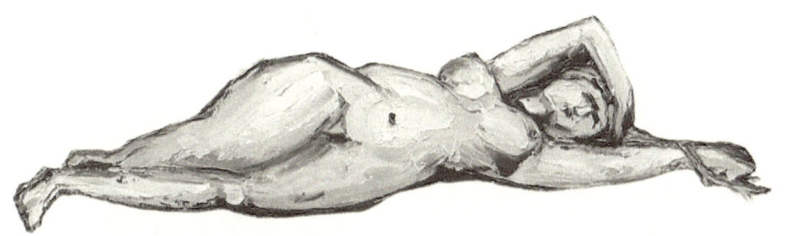

GROTESQUE SINGERS

RICK MULLIN

DOS MADRES

2025

DOS MADRES PRESS INC.
P.O. Box 294, Loveland, Ohio 45140
www.dosmadres.com   editor@dosmadres.com

Dos Madres is dedicated to the belief that the small press is essential to the vitality of contemporary literature as a carrier of the new voice, as well as the older, sometimes forgotten voices of the past. And in an ever more virtual world, to the creation of fine books pleasing to the eye and hand.

Dos Madres is named in honor of Vera Murphy and Libbie Hughes, the "Dos Madres" whose support have made this press possible.

Dos Madres Press, Inc. is an Ohio Not For Profit Corporation and a 501 (c) (3) qualified public charity. Contributions are tax deductible.

Executive Editor: Robert J. Murphy

Illustration & Book Design: Elizabeth H. Murphy
www.illusionstudios.net

Cover painting: *The Birth of Venus after Cabanel*
by Rick Mullin. Oil on canvas, 26 x 40"

Author photo: Joe Muratore

Typeset in Adobe Garamond Pro & Sever
ISBN 978-1-962847-23-0
Library of Congress Control Number: 2025933905

ACKNOWLEDGEMENTS

I would like to thank the poets of Eratosphere for their friendship and skillful critique of new poems. Thanks to Hilary Sideris, David Katz, and Callen Michael Wesche, who read, or were read, poems in the manuscript, for their encouragement. Thanks also to my friend and longtime copy editor, Michele Arboit, whose attentive eye is unmatched.

Much gratitude to Robert and Elizabeth Murphy of Dos Madres Press.

Thanks and love always to Maureen, Emily, Maggie, and Lydia for their love and constant support.

I would also like to thank the editors of the following publications in which poems in *Grotesque Singers* have appeared: *Bad Lillies, Panorama, The High Window, Autumn Sky Poetry Daily,* and *Boog City*.

"Night" received first place in the Sonnet Crown category of the 2025 Kim Bridgford Memorial Sonnet Contest sponsored by Poetry by the Sea. Thanks to the 2025 contest judge, Austin Allen, and to the Poetry by the Sea conference organizers, Anna M. Evans, Nicole Caruso Garcia, and Linda Stern.

Dedicated to the memory of
Audrey Muratore & Kevin Jude Blewitt

TABLE OF CONTENTS

THE LOWING ANGELS AT THE DOOR

OBSERVE THE TIME

AN ATONAL ISLAND'S CHORD

THE TIDES THAT RISE AND FALL

GROTESQUE SINGERS

THE LOWING ANGELS
AT THE DOOR

Black Box

The dream in which your father reappears
is recognizably a stage device.
The wound that opens on your hand declaims
its monologue of apricot and stone
around a knee-high stack of paperbacks
you never cracked. Familiar European
cities spurn their fire codes and burn
into a narrow street, a black hotel,
the dream in which your lover calls once more.

Of course, you will remember that we're wired
to forget the plastic jug she filled
with something secret she refused to share.
You'll never have to cry with her again.
She's gone for good. Your notebook is a blank
except for where you try to take it down.
No reckoning, no measure will contain
your mystery. The plane that crashes time
and time again is nowhere to be found.

NIGHT

Every angel is terrifying ~ Rainer Maria Rilke

When I opened for Los Dildos at the Y,
I knew I'd get my ass kicked. They had horns
and huge cojones. And a different guy
on drums. Their singer wore a crown of thorns
(a little heavy on the metaphor)
and introduced himself as Caliban.
"This isn't going to be your night," he said.
He grabbed a cold one from the garbage can
and greened-out where the spotlight turns to red.
Establishing the five chord on the four,
I couldn't feel the strings. I let it slide.
The loners at the bar looked good to go—
the singer's girlfriend actually cried.
I heard the one-time drummer moanin' low
beside the lowing Angels at the door.

Beside the lowing Angels at the door
you have, of course, the Calibaniere,
fallen rebels sliding on the floor
who failed in flight. Their pain is temporary,
captured nonetheless in full effect.
Brueghelian bounce and broken bouncers all.
The emblematic owl and dragon's claw
depict the prosecution of a fall.
One bloated fish, one lion down by law,
whereat we pause a moment to reflect.
[beat]
They had another guy on drums. And horns
to make the high notes in a wamups scree

go *bang*; a porkpie hat that now adorns
a lady tattooed with a burning tree,
the girlfriend in a garden of neglect.

The girlfriend in a garden of neglect
(*pure* metaphor) arrived from Cincinnati,
swine metropolis in retrospect,
in 1984, done up in khaki.
But she wore an angel's shoes that matched
her Ellingtonian reserve and poise.
She said it without *saying* it so much.
No flags. The art world was a den of boys
to which the girlfriend brought a mother's touch.
And soon enough the Dildos were attached.
She worked them from the bar, gray eminence;
she fed them lines and also counted off.
A band of less experience than innocence
was coming off like Rimsky-Korsakov.
But there was yet a dragon to be hatched.

The basilisk, the one that hadn't hatched,
greened out inside its color-coded shell:
the mind of Caliban was jerry-patched
to mask his orchestrated dives to hell.
A drum and bass were moving in the pocket.
Everything was tight, but rotting from within.
A flatted four defined the outer reach,
constraining Aldo Klein on mandolin.
The paradox of Einstein on the beach:
The golden egg parabola, a locket
and the "ain't no lines in nature" jive
suggest the "Quandrum of the Other Side."

A message from the bar read *slide to five*.
The rhythm section shuddered and complied
as Larry on guitar got up to rock it.

When Larry on guitar sets up to rock it,
everything goes blue. His Reverb amp
defies the static and the thunder. Clock it,
measure every bar. It's true. The stamp
of time, the edge of irony. The howl.
He puts it down. To wit, that night in Dallas,
Pennsylvania, where the sidewalk stops:
The Pentecostals in a pine board palace
up the street immediately called the cops
when Larry bade his Telecaster growl.
That weekend in the can was a constraint
that failed to formulate a roadhouse yell.
But time inside is time inside. "There ain't
no lines in nature, boys. It's just as well,"
said Larry, turbaned in a jailhouse towel.

A turbine engine and a jailhouse towel.
A roadmap conjuring the big Midwest.
An Indiana flatness, hidden waterfowl
and more explosive elements to test
the mettle of a heavy metal band.
The burning Buddha and a burning man
in grapple stance and not-too-phony smoke
require the guidance of a dragoman
for any life form at the edge. A cloak
of darkness closeted in sunlit sand
on either coast completes the border wall.
And there you have it. Dildos hit the stage

in battle garb, in ink and alcohol.
You dig? Or do you simply turn the page
and carry on with life as you had planned?. . .

I carried on with life as I had planned,
a solo act: harmonica, guitar,
the occasional hurdy-gurdy, alto and
recorder. Once (and only once) sitar.
They'd thrown me out of Nouvelle Pomp the day
our debut album dropped. I got the "new
direction" kiss-off. "Any would suffice,"
I mocked, and packed my yellow Subaru.
That album, *Pfrank*, included "Edelweiss,"
my ode to white. It doesn't get much play
on college radio. Perhaps that's good—
I kinda like it when they draw a blank.
A multi-instrumentalist, I stood
alone on stage, resigned to putting *Pfrank*
behind me at the Uphill Cabaret.

Behind me at the Uphill Cabaret
a Fender Reverb Twin, the amplifier
Larry lugged along the motorway
when Everyman was living on a tire
and (surprisingly, foreshadowing. . .) a prayer.
I recognized the axman's signature,
"*Memento Mori*," burned into the vinyl—
The heavy-handed man's imprimatur,
the frank magnificence of all things final.
Those decals of the Dead and Slayer
were added by another hand. But whose?
And when? And why? "House amp," said a drummer

for the headline act, the Existential Blues.
"I guess the guy who owned it hit his number."
Well drummers come and go, but Larry is a player. . . .

Hell, drummers disappear! But Larry. . . is a player.
Unlikely he'd just suddenly decamp.
Los Dildos' patent leather lammergeier
would not abandon such a storied amp.
"How long has it been sitting there?" I asked.
But the Existential drummer was no more.
Alone on stage I thought about the crowd.
The crowd was waiting, heavy at the door.
The green room was beginning to get loud,
The Uphill Cabaret crew multitasked.
The night was good to go, and I went first.
I opened wide and closed with "Edelweiss."
The Existentials, likely unrehearsed,
started several numbers over twice.
The singer slouched in seraph feathers, masked.

Louche seraphim in feathers mask
the far basilica. The foreground dark,
the middle field, a hay-gold meadow, gasps
below the mountains and the sky. *"!Hark!"*
it prays. A novice monk replies in kind,
his lute communicating with angelic strings
just out of hearing range. *Memento Mori*
reads a cloud line band. The novice sings
a new rendition of the same old story:
Our hero leaves his Fender amp to find
a better stage, a more receptive base.
The landscape is a dream within a dream.

The hooded novice doesn't show his face.
In landscape paintings, no one hears you scream.
Not so in the cathedral of the mind.

And so, the green cathedral of the mind,
the pentagram that Leonardo drew,
a canticle uncannily designed
for human voice and playing through,
inverted with the head of Baphomet:
Thus Caliban, unfettered and unplugged,
Vitruvian in burning forest green,
a basilisk in smoke, alive and drugged,
emerges from the oriental screen
and lunges through the Dildos' second set,
no longer shadow play.
                              [More light. More light . . .]
Then counting off (and counting up to five),
he howls, "This isn't going to be your day!"
Or is it night? Again the Dildos come alive,
Promethean. This isn't over yet.

The problem is, this isn't over yet.
We haven't seen the last of Nouvelle Pomp ~
their sophomore outing, *Balzac Tourniquet*,
sees action on the charts and at the Stomp.
And now that Brother Larry reads the sky,
he's likely to deliver on those psalms
he promised in his last encyclical.
There's little respite from the dry ice bombs
at Uphill Cabaret. Though not admissible,
the groaning testimony of the guy
who used to bang the drum portends a round

of rhythm section shuffle, and the girlfriend's
tears may show up in the lost and found.
It's sloppy. But my reminiscence ends
the night I opened for Los Dildos at the Y.

CORRECTING THE PORTRAIT

Extinguishing Clausen's divine tongue of light
with a hammer and chisel. It still isn't right.

Victoria's aura, in need of repair,
comes down to the question of halo or hair.

Katrina was happy with sitting for hours.
We'll add bitter rue to her tin can of flowers.

I managed to pen-in a session with Rose
whose spirit evades me. That's life, I suppose. ~

One sitter objected to what *Matisse* drew.
Matisse said, "It isn't a picture of you."

Picasso delivered a similar line
when met with demurrals from one Gertrude Stein.

That's after he'd scraped off a third of her face,
brought it home and re-scumbled his own in its place.

THE OBSCURE

"Everything else can wait." ~ George Harrison

Trapped in a world, a world he never made,
no wonder he was called the quiet one.
He slept with every instrument he played.
He wasn't what you'd call a lot of fun,
he wasn't in it for the Revolution.
In separating art from politics
he placed no stock in politics per se.
He laid his burden on a bed of sticks
and timpani. The bells rang breakaway.
Religion on a field of Evolution.
He danced among the consorts of the Lord
and photographed their gardens in the fall,
expressing his devotion. There's a chord
that's seldom heard, responding to a call.
A gesture that defies a resolution.

My Shot at Jesus

When John McMenamin demurred—they say
he didn't want to wear his mother's gown—
I got my shot at Jesus. We were down
to just a week before the Easter Play.

St. Rose of Lima's pageant was about
as close as you could get to by-the-book.
The script was written by a crew that took
the Bible to my room and knocked it out.

I'd wear a sheet. When Judas kissed my cheek
(McMenamin objection number two)
I'd be uncomfortable, but I'd get through.
I'd drag the cardboard cross. I wouldn't speak.

Then Andrea Tartaglia would lift
the face of Christ drawn on a handkerchief.

OBSERVE THE TIME

Pictures at an Exhibition

I - The Rictus Wheel
After Pieter Bruegel the Elder's The Triumph of Death

Your scepter and your armor and your gold
collide and clatter with the grinning bone
whose hourglass and sword will bleed you cold.

The rictus wheel sets high above the wold
where raptors of the burning lake are shown
your scepter and your armor and your gold.

The young will pile up sideways with the old
in sudden deference to the chaperone
whose pendulum and sword will bleed you cold.

A pit where your constituents are poled
guffaws beside the ruins of your throne.
Your scepter and your armor and your gold

add color to the weary soul you sold.
It hangs in the Museo del Jamón
where standing time and sword will bleed you cold.

The thin men of Adipocere and Mold
roll everywhere. Cry foul? You'll cry alone.
Your scepter and your armor and your gold,
your sundial and your sword, will bleed you cold.

II - Odds

After Albert Pinkham Ryder's The Race Track (Death on a Pale Horse)

The odds are in your favor, yet the same.
The house is under camp smoke. But it's there.
Of course the serpent startles at the game.

O clockwise rider, you are not to blame.
Smart money isn't always on the square.
The odds are in your favor, yet the same—

a tablespoon of absinthe set aflame,
a cloud line hammered tight enough to tear.
Of course the serpent startles at the game.

The morning after doesn't fit the frame,
no upshot in the echo of despair.
The odds are in your favor, yet the same,

candescent jockey. Psychopomp by name.
The remit of your landscape, laissez-faire.
Of course the serpent startles at the game.

The hour you present the winning claim
is tolled in rolling numbers, fog and prayer.
The odds are in your favor, yet the same.
Of course the serpent startles at the game.

III - PANTOMIME

After J.M.W. Turner's Death on a Pale Horse

Azrael comes charging through the lime
and kiln smoke. Glorious in red he rides,
a gladiator in a Roman pantomime.

Miasma bleeds quinacridone and grime,
the battlefield exhales triglycerides.
Azrael comes charging through the lime,

an echo of the dying Gaul in slime
and agony whose tortured frame elides
the gladiator in a Roman pantomime,

our claustrophobic nightmares, and a crime
against humanity. He writhes and slides.
Azrael comes charging through the lime,

a rack of venison at Christmastime.
He gestures in the air of Ironsides,
a gladiator in a Roman pantomime.

Struck-dumb soliloquy in perfect rhyme,
the death rasp of the King of Suicides.
Azrael comes charging through the lime,
a gladiator in Roman a pantomime.

FLORIDIAN

The stewards of this ball park actually keep
a dirty vat of swarming ray fish to amuse
the fans. Black wings challenging the dreck
of concrete bleachers and rotating advertisement.
One almost admires the conservative, clean-shaven
Yankee players in their orderly progress from field
to dugout, each setting an example at the plate.
A Prussian rectitude incapable of forgiveness
registers in the boxes as does the prospect
of a no-hitter well toward evening. Nonetheless,
both teams fall apart in the seventh inning.
The game becomes annoyingly interesting
as bases load and powder kegs go boom.
The sun sets citrus orange over Tampa Bay,
where nothing can renew the breeze of nothing.

COMMISSION TO PAINT A SAPLING IN THE PARK

I'll have to go to Edvard Munch on this.
And Henrik Ibsen, channeling the North,
its atmospheric gestures, stony words
with adamant varietals for God
and Hell. I'll have to lie down in the grass
and hide the sky behind a linden row
and dig it out and find a place for such
a tiny stalk, its yellow leaves turned down.
A daughter's tree exulting in a time
before experience. A hidden lamp,
an April field that trails into the mist.
I must consult the masters, find the way
to render something chained to memories
that map onto a strange imagination.

PARIS QUALITY

Split Eights,
Exchange Place, Manhattan

She lays out Paris-quality croissants.
I'd suffer anything. I'd stand in line
and pay the price. A heart wants what it wants.

I'm weary of the railroad restaurants,
the cardboard cakes, the neon anodyne.
She lays out Paris-quality croissants,

her hidden smile a Harlem Renaissance.
She's elegant. I'm old. If she were mine,
I'd pay the price. A heart wants what it wants.

Her music wakens me, the darkness haunts.
I'm running late as always, which is fine.
She lays out Paris-quality croissants

and conjures coffee for the dilettantes
through steam and ritual. It's after nine?
I'll pay the price. A heart wants what it wants

and finds its way regardless of the consequences,
unrestrained and borderline.
She lays out Paris-quality croissants.
I'll pay the price. A heart wants what it wants.

BLUES

The saxophone I never learned to play
is held up at the factory for good.
The bus to where I never used to stay
is burning in a rundown neighborhood.
I'm blowing payday on a New York wine.

The paper napkin symphony I penned
is soaking in the tub and wearing thin.
I'm fishing for a thesis to defend
(my annotated *Huckleberry Finn*
was canceled by Millennials online).

The altarpiece I wasn't paid to paint
is somewhere in the basement at the back.
It's short beatitudes. I'm down a saint.
It's varnished, but I'm waiting for a crack
so I can start to scrape it back to pine.

MR. MACHINE

A devil-red development for boys
endowed with a transparent gearbox chest,
he masters locomotion and destroys
the world. Of all my toys, I love him best,
this robot golem of the living room.
His top hat makes it clear that he's in charge,
his crooked grin both sinister and wise.
A wind-up evolution while at large,
he makes the day seem plausible. His eyes
foresee the perfect future. I resume
on track behind his cranky adamant
advance. It hurts to put the man away.
I'd like to say I know him. But I can't.
I *trust* him as I trust the state of play
at Ideal Toys, the architects of doom.

Tattoo Man

In Memoriam

Gone the days of Polaroid April sunshine,
sacrosanct Memorial Day encounters;
Pinewood Derbies, Rotary potluck dinners,
dollar-sign notebooks.

Now the taste of something unlike tomorrow.
Now a rage subliminal to the suburbs.
Promise made, an endless excuse delivered.
Enter a stranger

marked for life, thrown out of the Caldwell Diner,
pinched at Jack's while squeezing the pomegranate.
Bounced from bars, a put-upon Queequeg doling
infinite cowboy.

"Holy Mack'rel, even the face, Paulina!"
Hauling arms a coloratura ocean.
Here be dragons. There a peculiar shade of
prodigal lodger.

You'll recall. You called the police, remember?
Shielded children, shocked when you saw him coming?
Now your white Republican enclave shimmers.
Down in the summer

news comes slow: A lull in the Captain's Tower.
Valerie and Vivian stack the tray for
tickets to the Teenage Patrolman's Breakfast.
Aren't we happy.

DRUMMER

The metal you reach, the moments you crash,
the muscle you lay into playing for cash,
the feelings you hope you might one day express,
your gift and your eminent grab (more or less)
determine the sprawl and the shape of your pocket,

the tilt of your swing, the ball in you socket,
the shine of your skin, the height of your chair,
the twist of the keys on the side of your snare,
the hole in your bass, the decades of wear
and a feeling that comes from the-devil-knows-where
with the mass dissolution of most of your gear,

the darkness of dancers, the silence you find
in the hall of confession, the back of your mind,
the pace of your heart, the staggering light,
the small kit required for keeping it tight
and an echo of lines you may one day recite
in the studio space of the oncoming night.

FORTINBRAS

Come make your closing song, O worthy foe,
last hero in the quiver of my foils.
Produce the fire mop and let us know
the profile of the victor and his spoils.
Extinguish every light along your way.
True comedy is tragedy, a fact
that few indeed are willing to exploit.
I tried. You should have seen the second act
last summer in the wings at Bayreuth.
Remind us that the thing is still a play
in which you're mentioned maybe once or twice.
Remember that there is no guarantee.
The stage goes dark, it's embers turn to ice.
Observe the time. Arrive and speak for me
before you're canceled by Olivier.

AN ATONAL ISLAND'S CHORD

THE LOST BOAT

I

According to my notes, a ten-percent-
illuminated waxing gibbous moon
was all we had to work with. It would do.
The sea lay still, a silver firmament
of undulating stars; the last harpoon
lay dark and cold, the compass black and blue.
He pulled a quadrant from his leather sack
and smiled. "Science ruins everything."
A band of crimson bled upon the line.
As he prepared to work his metal gage,
the clouds engaged the East in coloring
a burning sky, the ancient warning sign.
I made another entry on the page.
The ink ran wet, illegible and black.

II

The ink ran wet, indelible and black.
My charts inevitably wandered south.
Behind my apple blossom barricade,
the words fell into pictures. To a stack
of portraits with a problem at the mouth.
I studied Audubon—the garden weighed
a ton. I thought about the world outside,
three quarters of it under water. Wet,
indelible and black, my observations
dried to crack. I needed to get out
into the violent landscape, take my set
of facts into the world of conversations
and calamities. I watched the sky. I thought about
the hills. I contemplated suicide.

III

The hills are contemplating suicide
in all her pictures. Color conjures latent
earthquakes harmonized in russet gold
and green. Her heavy swaths of black collide
with barren trees at the horizon. Blatant
heart attacks beneath the surface fold
into the dark impasto of her palette knife.
"A heavy calm," I whispered as we stood
before what I would call her masterpiece.
She looked away. "It's coming, but it's slow."
A large scale canvas of an autumn wood
at sundown startled by a shock of geese
in V formation. "It's a late Rousseau,"
I said. "It brings that hidden world to life."

IV

We sought to bring the hidden world to life
in underground repositories, day
and night describing novel specimens
we'd gathered in the field from Tenerife
to Nova Scotia northward all the way
to Greenland. To the Arctic Circle. Tens
of thousands—vertebrate, invertebrate,
the avian, marine and microscopic.
Flamboyant drinkers, egotists, the men
who'd boost America from mole
to Megatherium! Our philanthropic
vessel on the Mall was listing then,
a New World Tower of Babel on the whole,
yet somehow managing to compensate.

V

"We're somehow managing to compensate,"
Eduardo said, while lighting his cigar.
"The Royal Society is getting old.
And Harvard's Agassiz will soon debate
this Darwin fellow." "*There's* a rising star,"
I said. "His *Origin of the Species* sold
at least a hundred copies Friday night."
"But there are other ways of measuring
success, my friend. And other ways to skin
a cod." The waiter brought another round.
"I'll be in Boston. We'll be treasuring
comparative zoology's big win
next Saturday. Might you be on the ground?"
At three-pints-in I shook my head. "I might."

VI

At three-pints-in I shook my head. "I might
delay my trip for this," "You can't," said Jane.
"Your paper. And you'd miss the grand debates."
"I'll miss the debut of your landscape at that flight
of marble stairs. Let's read this once again:
*Beyond America the World Awaits
the National Academy Reception,*"
a headline to the notice that a star,
a woman nonetheless, holds center stage
among the bearded stalwarts. "And you depart
New Bedford Tuesday," she replied. Thus far
I had a second working title page:
*New Journey to the Turning Roads in Art
and Natural History.* A modest misconception.

VII

" 'Natural History, our model for perception,
renders clarity from chaos...' " "Order,"
said Eduardo. "Look for systems, not
for inspiration. Matter of perception,
so to speak. But still, as a recorder
of our field discoveries a lot
of what you'll draw are diagrams. Instead
of pictures, think of charts and maps.
That goes for anatomical display."
"But there are gestures, there are hidden lines
we measure more in sympathy." "Perhaps."
He smiled. "You've told me all about 'the way
of seeing.' " "Symbols, metaphor, and signs..."
"Remember: Objectivity!" he said.

VIII

"Remember! Objectivity!" I said,
"The sea engenders optical illusion."
"Yes, and science ruins everything!"
That smile again, the cloud line flowing red
behind his silhouetted frame. "Confusion
crowned as my confession, I shall sing
the sundown gray!" And so we played our game,
our voices interchangeable. Our tools
laid out before us, elegant and brutal
included whaling weapons used to tag
leviathan anomalies. The rules
of the New England fisheries are futile
in a shiver of Atlantic sharks. Bag
the specimen, number it by name.

IX

Bag the specimen, number it by name
and color it by lamplight down below.
The amber highlights of a Barbizon
oak forest with a soft October flame
behind the cracking wall, the subtle glow
of an eternity on fire.... Carry on.
I carried on, a picture in my brain
that bled into my final color sketch
of *Sepia apama,* the frozen sealife
anchoring my brown anatomy
and book of numbers. I would stretch
a canvas broader than a sail to knife
the dark impasto of a dead academy
were I to pay anatomy in kind.

X

Were I to pay anatomy in kind,
I'd take an oarsman's seat aboard this skiff
and pull against the waves with all my might.
Instead I settle in the saltwash, blind
behind my barricade of hieroglyph
and calculation. Odd. An anchorite.
The Dolphin lowered its intrepid craft
at noon, each headed in a different direction.
I boarded with Eduardo on the largest boat,
preparing tackle for the bowhead whale
we hoped to tag, and kit for the collection
of green algae and crustaceans set afloat
behind an undulating mammal's tail.
I'd taken my assigned position aft.

XI

I'd taken my assigned position aft.
Eduardo stood beside the single mast
on which a yellow canvas sail ballooned.
The oarsmen rested as a summer draft
propelled the jolly boat until at last
a white explosion and a moaning tuned
to some unearthly pitch. Our rising prey
appeared and disappeared. As did our ship,
The Dolphin. Dropping sail, the crew began
to pull the oars. Eduardo threw the trawling
nets and shouted orders to the crew. "Let's whip
this animal! Make ready with the lances, man."
He jostled the harpooner. "Keep it hauling!"
The surface broke again in teeming spray.

XII

The surface broke again in teeming spray
illuminated by the bleeding sun,
its amber light in torrents shot with green.
A mortal chaos turning. Judgement Day
at the academy, a metric ton
of oil on canvas and a magazine
exploding all along our ardent keel.
The forest burning over marble stairs
of endless arguments that tend to sink.
The tearing of the sixth or seventh seal,
unrecognizable, with unseen flares
exploding canvas reams of carbon ink
that explicate the world to some extent—
according to my notes, at ten percent.

PHTHALOCYANINE

Between Cities

The Hudson, blue now as the glassy shore,
resolves to an atonal island's chord,
a boat-length segment of the atmosphere.
One trader falls into the morning wind,
alarming echoes in the ferry wake.

Another stranger on her telephone
may not be one of several women seen
dissolving in the Saturday cafes.
A piece of everything fits nicely here.
The towers shine. A few of them have wings.

After All

So here we are, abandoned after all.
The institute of art and science leans
its cannon on the clouds. Its blackened windows
catch the secondary harmonies converging
into gray, aspiring to titanium.
Our friends are working in remote locations,
vaccinated. The inoculated city
after all. We read about the war
on sheets of ice, communicating care
on silicon devices. Towers disappear
in this vicinity, they always have.
A quarter note once rose above the hole
that runs uptown. It disappeared again.
The skylights can't remember anything,
and here we are in twilight after all.

Astor Place,
New York City
2022

FIRINGS

An e-mail greeted me at 9 am
delivered from my own address. It claimed
my laptop had been commandeered, allowing
hackers to deploy the camera, and thus
a video exists of my activity
in sync with the associated "content".
It gave me 50 hours, 2 days plus,
to pay $800, warning not
to pass the message on to anyone,
reminding me the clock was started
when I opened the transparent threat.
Of course, they had the contact information
handy to destroy my reputation....
I turned the message in at Systems Help.

At 10 am, another message with
a reconfigured org chart and a screen
of jargon, ending on a heartless note:
"We say goodbye to Stephanie Puleo."

Outside the Stock Exchange, a Christmas tree
insists upon its ideal cone of light
illuminating nothing. *Fearless Girl,*
abandoned in a shadowy December
afternoon, stands adamant. Embronzed.
Thank God they didn't leave her at the bull.

I'm hoping to be gone before such thoughts
come audible at Broad Street and Exchange,
the crossroads of a crowded finance zone

where I observe the time and contemplate
the bannered columns, armored cars, the sun
relentless, and the consequence of flight.

SEINE

Conjuring the palette of old Pissarro,
river's edge, the moon in its veil of powder
blue, my constant wandering headed nowhere,
you are beside me

here and gone, a ghost in October yellow,
molded shade that covers abandoned bookstalls,
mon amie, immaculate carbon footprint,
burning cathedral.

ON THE DEATH OF ANONYMOUS

A master of negative space,
remember him
not for object

but for gesture
in a wake where he moved
through the world.

Assume the shape
of his imagination,
the backlight of his dream,

his preference for color
over line.

Find poetry in the act
of making language
disappear.

THE TIDES THAT RISE AND FALL

Expression (Sunset) or the Death of Venus

The products of combustion are contained
in brickwork vaults designed by engineers
adept at solitude, their fire explained
in darkness. Our intrepid gondoliers
inspect the morning from a high balloon
recording trace emissions in a code
reengineered from signals in the war.
No reason for the Peaceful Valley to explode.
In fact, we needn't worry anymore
about the Human Epoch, which is soon
or maybe later to dissolve in light.
The constellation Pisces will unwind
its net of epithelia and kite
in two directions, leaving us behind.
The pond was deathly still this afternoon.

The pond was deathly still this afternoon
as William pulled his shopping cart behind
a backstop in the park. A powder moon
accompanied his daydream in the blind
and covered up his song like no tomorrow.
They say it never comes, yet there's a scene
in William's history that proves he's way
ahead and wrapped in polyethylene.
Tomorrow is a glass on yesterday
where nothing happens. We're inclined to borrow,
singing hardship forward in a line
with gladness, twinning elements of drool
and drama that inscribe a 69,
a yin and yang, a chiral molecule
impervious to all the moon can sorrow.

Impervious to all the moon can sorrow,
frozen mountains slam their wood-crack strains.
All color drained, gone even from the dayglow
factories that burned once and their trains
that throttled through the county night and day.
A river choked with yellow nurdles plies
the fallen forest like a mindless snail.
The sun appears, but always in disguise,
and disappears. We're startled by a pale
hypocrisy that jumps across the clay
to hobble back into the shadow twist
and bracken fall. Consult the lying stars
regarding our domain. Consult the mist
that folds them in obscurity with Mars
and Venus, who were always in the way.

When Venus, who was always in the way,
employed the reptile cure, her arrow boys
became undisciplined. Their hate held sway;
green eyes gone lightless as their feathered toys
collected dust. Nothing slowed them down.
The god of combat, in his bleeding cape
of mercury and sulfur, had a war
to angle, and a trial to escape
(coincident convenience), and a score
to settle, and a gathering in town
of arrow boys. The table's set. Regard
his vanguard in the gutter and a staff
of banners flapping with his limp petard.
There is no ending to the epitaph
he needs to write. He needs to write a crown.

He needs to write a 16-sonnet crown
of sonnets to revive an atrophied
imagination. He needs to paint a clown
in order to recharge his palette, plant a seed.
Ontogeny might recapitulate
phylogeny. It's happened once before.
Today, the page defines an empty frame,
a canvas primed and white. The killing metaphor,
an outcome predetermined. All the same,
he rises, careful not to saturate
the grays, and draws a bass drum for the boom
of brave Pierrot. He'll stand him tall beside
the plaque that reads *Cogito, ergo sum*.
Accordion and mandolin provide
A melody that carries on 'til late.

A melody that carries on 'til late
will likely nibble, as Ouroboros,
a tail familiar with the grass; a great
awakening to visions of morose
encounters in the past. A balance sheet.
Reminders of an echoed reckoning
of glory days in ashed recrimination.
Aubade, all good and ugly, beckoning
like Ahab in the motion picture adaptation.
O, the worm returns, a Hollywood conceit.
God help us. We won't bother You again.
Just get us out of this, Who put us here,
and let us be. Sélah. Shalom. Amen.
Or write us headlines for a winning year
to read, resist, forget, recast, repeat.

Recast, resist, forget, rewrite, repeat
the Protocols of Zion while the God of War
renews his contract with a non-compete.
He plays the numbers at a liquor store,
returning home to phone in his report,
though lately he's been interviewed on Zoom
by operatives who cover up his game
for networks on the left. His living room
suggests he's off the wagon, and the shame
is amplified by questions from a court
reporter in New York. His latest book,
in garish product placement, fills a quarter
of the screen. He acts if he's somehow off the hook
when asked of the condition of his daughter.
"War," he pleads, "is endless. Life is short."

Remember brutish, nasty, poor and short?
Well that's the guy who got us here, correct?
An agent of the Age of Light, a sort
of demagogue whose ironies reflect
grave error through a veil of time release.
Who made *him* God? [...The men of modern science
in cahoots with industry and government.]
The hoi polloi react in big defiance
and its outrage kind of cracks the firmament.
The cracking mountains slam, the southward geese
describe another airborne letter: Q.
Our gondoliers recalibrate the glass
that measures complements of CO_2.
The little guy yells, "Blow it out your ass."
Sing War is Over (If You Want It). Peace.

La Déesse Morte sings, "If you want it, peace
comes dropping slow." Beside her rings the snake
that laid her low. Below, the blood and grease
repel in tinted jewels and rainbow flake,
an image in a leaded window, stained,
desiring only fire (see Stanza One
to find the definition). William sleeps
beneath his cart, protected from the sun
that burns a pathway through the park and keeps
the promise of a paradise regained.
The networks in their perfect opposition
fill the hour with a tired spin
as engineers review the composition
of a brickwork archbasilica wherein
the products of combustion are contained.

GRAVITY

My mother, made inert by weight and knee,
spends waking hours watching her TV.
The laptop she obtained on QVC
lies dark and out of reach, predictably.
We call, but all her calls are transferred straight
to voicemail. She doesn't read. She stays up late.
The only stimulant she has to compensate
for everything she's blocked is solid state
illumination (decorative notions,
side effect disclaimers, jewelry promotions…)
Her dreams must bear a weight of lost emotions.
She sleeps. And when she wakes she thinks of oceans.
She lies in bed and tries to name them all.
But some are seas, perhaps. She can't recall.
She thinks about the tides that rise and fall.
She'd like a globe, she tells me. Something small.

Aubade

Now the winds of April exhume a morning
shorn of mist. Unreasoning breaks the daylight.
Echoed strains of *Horowitz Plays Scriabin*
cool in the ashes.

I'm awake. The coffee decants in Pyrex.
Clouds break down as newspapers skid the driveways
out along the boulevard of contrition.
God isn't watching,

you're asleep. The radio, jammed on zero,
still complains how one is a lonely number.
I'm OK. In deep with the mug's imbalance.
Nothing is final.

GREEN GIANTS

Reading Yakovlev and watching birds,
distracted by the flight-line of a bee,
I'm not expected to remember words
or recognize a new variety
of arborvitae when the hemlocks die.
They're popular and bound to fill the space
in which my neighbor's outdoor television
chips away at memory. The grace
notes fade into a faltering retention.
And now the dove has fixed its amber eye,
the window to a winter soul, on mine.
My afternoon of tea and chlorophyll
dissolves into the halo of a pine
that something in the yard forgot to kill,
a tea stain on the border of the sky.

SUTRA

Today the fox in muffled morning light
appears near death himself. His rodent prey
hangs listless from his jaws. He notices
my eye but doesn't skip a stolen beat
in his retreat through smoke that filters down
from Nova Scotia. He knows we're near the end.
Which reminds me, we must kill our mentors
on the astral plane. Extract their many voices,
bury them with their eyes. Erase their judgement.
Nothing should remain of their indulgence.
Which reminds me of a clouded peak,
an aphorism written on the sun,
a sudden wind that tells you what you know.

BAILEY

I'd call the operation on your leg
a Pyrrhic victory. It fixed the tear,
but left you with a twisted gait. And pain.
An animal with 15 years at best,
you seemed to jump from 4 to maybe 10.
I let you hobble in a fenced-in yard.
Like me, you have a problem with the neighbors.

Today, beneath the hemlock tree, we find
a softball frozen in the winter mud.
I kick it loose and toss it on the grass.
Of course you chase it through the ragged shadows,
overshoot and hunker back. You nearly
swallow it. Above us in the blue
two urban raptors circle toward the sun.

ABOUT THE AUTHOR

RICK MULLIN is a painter and writer living in northern New Jersey. His poetry has appeared in various journals and anthologies including *American Arts Quarterly, The New Criterion, Measure, The Raintown Review, Ep;phany, Bad Lillies, Unsplendid*, and *Rabbit Ears: TV Poems*. His books include *Soutine* (Dos Madres, 2012), *Sonnets from the Voyage of the Beagle* (Dos Madres, 2014), *Lullaby and Wheel* (Kelsay Books, 2019), and *Huncke* (second edition, Exot Books, 2021). His paintings are in collections in the U.S., Canada, England, Germany, Italy, Greece, the Netherlands, the British Virgin Islands and Australia.

www.ingramcontent.com/pod-product-compliance
Lightning Source LLC
Chambersburg PA
CBHW020334130626
46549CB00003B/1179